# Joint Response by the Inspectors General of the Department of the Treasury and Board of Governors of the Federal Reserve System

*Request for Information Regarding the Bureau of Consumer Financial Protection*

January 10, 2011

OIG-CA-11-004
FRB OIG 2011-01

The Honorable Spencer Bachus
Chairman
Committee on Financial Services

The Honorable Judy Biggert
Chairman
Committee on Financial Services, Subcommittee
   on Insurance, Housing and Community Opportunity

U.S. House of Representatives
2129 Rayburn House Office Building
Washington, DC 20515

Dear Chairman Bachus and Chairman Biggert:

This letter and its enclosure respond to your November 22, 2010, request for
information concerning the Department of the Treasury's (Treasury) activities to
establish the Bureau of Consumer Financial Protection (Bureau).

In preparing our response, we (1) reviewed the applicable sections of the Dodd-
Frank Wall Street Reform and Consumer Protection Act and other relevant laws and
(2) requested, obtained, and reviewed relevant information and documentation from
Treasury and the Board of Governors of the Federal Reserve System. In addition,
we interviewed key Treasury officials including: the Assistant to the President and
Special Advisor to the Secretary of the Treasury on the Consumer Financial
Protection Bureau, Treasury's General Counsel, the Chief of Staff of the Bureau
Implementation Team, the Deputy Assistant Secretary for Management and
Budget, and the Director of the Office of Financial Management.

As a courtesy, we provided the Treasury Deputy Secretary with a draft of this
letter and its enclosure and considered Treasury's comments as we prepared the
final document.

Page 2

We are sending a similar letter to the Honorable Barney Frank, Ranking Member.

We would be pleased to brief you or members of your staffs on this material or any other work under our respective or joint jurisdictions. If you have any questions, you may contact us at (202) 622-1090 (Inspector General Eric M. Thorson), or at (202) 973-5000 (Inspector General Elizabeth A. Coleman). In addition, a member of your staff may contact Marla A. Freedman, Assistant Inspector General for Audit, Treasury Office of Inspector General, at (202) 927-5400, or Jacqueline M. Becker, Associate Inspector General for Legal Services, Board of Governors of the Federal Reserve System Office of Inspector General, at (202) 973-5045.

Sincerely,


/s/                                          /s/

Eric M. Thorson                              Elizabeth A. Coleman
Inspector General                            Inspector General
Department of the Treasury                   Board of Governors of the Federal Reserve
                                             System


Enclosure

**Joint Response by the Inspectors General of the Department of the Treasury and Board of Governors of the Federal Reserve System**

*Request for Information Regarding the Bureau of Consumer Financial Protection*

---

## A. Transparency

1. *While the interim authority of the Bureau lies with Treasury, who is responsible for exercising the role of Inspector General – the Federal Reserve OIG or Treasury's OIG?*

   Both the Office of Inspector General (OIG) for the Board of Governors of the Federal Reserve System (Board) and the OIG for the Department of the Treasury (Treasury) have a role in overseeing the Bureau of Consumer Financial Protection (Bureau) during the interim period. Under provisions of the Dodd-Frank Wall Street Reform and Consumer Protection Act (Dodd-Frank Act), the Board's Inspector General is responsible for exercising the role of Inspector General for the Bureau. Specifically, the Dodd-Frank Act provides that the Board's Inspector General "shall have all of the authorities and responsibilities provided by [the Inspector General Act of 1978] with respect to the [Bureau], as if the Bureau were part of the [Board]." This provision became effective on the date of enactment. Moreover, Treasury OIG has authority to oversee the interim efforts to establish the Bureau because (1) Treasury has authority to conduct interim activities related to establishing the Bureau and (2) the Inspector General Act grants Treasury OIG the authority to conduct audits, investigations, and other reviews of Treasury's programs and operations.[1] The Board OIG and Treasury OIG plan to coordinate and cooperate on audits, inspections, and other reviews of the Bureau's operations, as appropriate.

2. *Has Secretary Geithner taken any steps, formally or informally, to delegate to any other person or persons the interim authority granted to him by Section 1066 of the Dodd-Frank Act? If so, please identify the person or persons, describe any delegation of authority or duties and provide copies of any document reflecting that delegation.*

---

[1] Treasury OIG's oversight authority does not include the Internal Revenue Service, which is under the jurisdictional oversight of the Treasury Inspector General for Tax Administration, or the Troubled Asset Relief Program (TARP), which is under the jurisdictional oversight of the Special Inspector General for the TARP.

**Joint Response by the Inspectors General of the Department of the Treasury and Board of Governors of the Federal Reserve System**

*Request for Information Regarding the Bureau of Consumer Financial Protection*

---

The interim authority contained in section 1066 of the Dodd-Frank Act is divided into two sections: section 1066(a) and section 1066(b). Section 1066(a) grants authority to the Secretary of the Treasury (Secretary) to perform the Bureau's functions included under subtitle F of title X of the Dodd-Frank Act. Prior to the designated transfer date, the functions of the Bureau under subtitle F include, among other things, the authority to (1) negotiate employee transfers with the transferring agencies; (2) carry out the provisions of subtitle F related to the compensation and benefits of those employees transferring to the Bureau; and (3) accompany the current federal regulators on consumer compliance examinations of large banks, savings associations, and credit unions. On the designated transfer date, however, the functions of the Bureau under subtitle F are expanded to include rulemaking, examination, and other functions that transfer to the Bureau from the other federal regulators. Section 1066(b) grants Treasury authority to perform "administrative services" in support of the Bureau.

Secretary Geithner delegated the interim authority granted to him under section 1066 of the Dodd-Frank Act to Professor Elizabeth Warren, in her role as Special Advisor to the Secretary, and other Treasury officials who are working to stand up the Bureau, design its structure, identify and hire staff, and set initial goals and priorities. According to Treasury's General Counsel, Treasury's organic statute, which defines the Department's general authorities, (1) permits the Secretary to delegate his authorities (in this case, the interim authority granted under section 1066), and (2) does not require documentation of such delegations.[2] Apart from standing delegation orders, Treasury officials told us that the delegation of the Secretary's interim authority under section 1066 has not been documented.

For matters related to funding the Bureau, Treasury and the Board executed an interagency agreement that identifies certain employees who are authorized to act in the Secretary's place and with his authority for designated activities. As part of this interagency agreement, Secretary Geithner authorized the following individuals to work with the Board on funding-related matters: Dan Tangherlini,

---

[2] 31 U.S.C. § 321(b)(2) (providing the Secretary's delegation authority).

**Joint Response by the Inspectors General of the Department of the Treasury and Board of Governors of the Federal Reserve System**

*Request for Information Regarding the Bureau of Consumer Financial Protection*

---

Assistant Secretary for Management and Chief Financial Officer; Adewale Adeyemo, Chief of Staff of the Bureau Implementation Team; Nani Coloretti, Deputy Assistant Secretary for Management and Budget; Elizabeth Erickson, Acting Chief Financial Officer of the Bureau Implementation Team; Dorrice Roth, Director, Office of Financial Management; and David Legge, Associate Director for Accounting, Office of Financial Management. The interagency agreement is provided as an Exhibit to this Enclosure.

3. *What oversight, if any, is Secretary Geithner (or anyone designated by Secretary Geithner) exercising with respect to (a) acts undertaken by others utilizing the interim authority conferred on the Treasury Secretary by Section 1066; and (b) proposals advanced by others with respect to use of that authority? Are Secretary Geithner or others within the Department able to exercise oversight effectively with respect to Professor Warren in light of her status as an Assistant to the President? As a practical matter, does that status preclude any oversight by anyone outside the White House?*

According to Treasury, when Professor Warren began her work on September 20, 2010, the Department put an oversight framework in place to provide for regular reviews of the implementation of the Bureau. These reviews include, but are not limited to, the following topics: policy priorities, the organizational design of the Bureau, resource allocation and budget, and decisions regarding personnel and hiring. As part of this process, Professor Warren has met regularly with the Secretary, Deputy Secretary, and other senior Treasury officials, including the Under Secretary for Domestic Finance, the Assistant Secretary for Financial Institutions, the Assistant Secretary for Management and Budget, the Chief of Staff, and the General Counsel. Treasury advised that over the course of this initial period, Professor Warren has met or talked by phone with the Secretary on at least seven separate occasions, including at least one private one-on-one meeting or call each month. She has met with the Deputy Secretary on at least eight separate occasions (three of which also included the Secretary). Treasury also advised that going forward, the Deputy Secretary has organized a regular, bi-weekly Bureau update meeting that will be attended by the Deputy Secretary, Professor Warren, other senior Treasury officials, and various members of the Bureau implementation team.

**Joint Response by the Inspectors General of the Department of the Treasury and Board of Governors of the Federal Reserve System**

*Request for Information Regarding the Bureau of Consumer Financial Protection*

---

Professor Warren stated that her role as an Assistant to the President is separate from her role as a Special Advisor to the Secretary. She explained that, as a Special Advisor to the Secretary, she is a full-time Treasury employee whose activities, which include periodically updating the President on the Bureau's implementation, are subject to the same oversight by the Secretary or his delegates afforded to any other Treasury official. She further noted that her role as an Assistant to the President does not preclude oversight related to her Bureau responsibilities. In describing her role as an Assistant to the President, Professor Warren stated that she speaks to the President and his advisors about issues that are not related to standing up the Bureau.

4. *Section 1100G of the Act requires the Bureau to describe the impact of any proposed rule on the cost of credit for small entities. Who will be in charge of conducting this analysis? Please provide descriptions of positions and the dates of hire for each Bureau staff person charged with conducting this analysis.*

The Bureau implementation team has not yet identified an individual(s) to conduct the analysis regarding the impact of any proposed rule on the cost of credit for small entities. Section 1100G, which requires the Bureau to perform this analysis, is not effective until the designated transfer date. Position description(s) for the individual(s) who will be conducting the analysis are not yet available. According to Treasury officials, the Bureau does not plan to propose any rules prior to the transfer date. Treasury officials further stated that they recognize that this is an important issue, and that the Bureau implementation team expects to review the issue carefully during the course of its future work.

5. *Do you agree that the interim authority specified in Section 1066 of the Act terminates on the designated transfer date, and that after such date, the Bureau can function only if a director has been confirmed with the advice-and-consent of the Senate?*

The interim authority specified in section 1066 of the Dodd-Frank Act does not fully terminate on the designated transfer date. Sections 1066(a) and 1066(b) identify two different expirations for Treasury's authority. The Secretary's

**Joint Response by the Inspectors General of the Department of the Treasury and Board of Governors of the Federal Reserve System**

*Request for Information Regarding the Bureau of Consumer Financial Protection*

---

authority under section 1066(a) terminates when a Director is confirmed by the Senate, rather than on the designated transfer date. Section 1066(a) states, "The Secretary is authorized to perform the functions of the Bureau under this subtitle *until the Director of the Bureau is confirmed by the Senate....*" In contrast, the authority of the Department of the Treasury under section 1066(b) terminates on the designated transfer date. Section 1066(b) states, "The Department of the Treasury may provide administrative services necessary to support the Bureau *before the designated transfer date.*"

If the Bureau does not have a Senate-confirmed Director by the designated transfer date, the Bureau may continue to operate under the Secretary's section 1066(a) authority. As discussed above, the Secretary's authority under section 1066(a) does not expire on the designated transfer date; instead, this authority continues until a Director is confirmed by the Senate. Specifically, until a Director is confirmed, section 1066(a) grants the Secretary the authority to carry out the functions of the Bureau found under subtitle F of title X.[3] On the designated transfer date, subtitle F grants the Bureau the authority to:

- prescribe rules, issue orders, and produce guidance related to the federal consumer financial laws that were, prior to the designated transfer date, within the authority of the Board, the Office of the Comptroller of the Currency, the Office of Thrift Supervision, the Federal Deposit Insurance Corporation, and the National Credit Union Administration;

- conduct examinations (for federal consumer financial law purposes) of banks, savings associations, and credit unions with total assets in excess of $10 billion, and any affiliates thereof;

- prescribe rules, issue guidelines, and conduct a study or issue a report (with certain limitations) under the enumerated consumer laws that were previously within the authority of the Federal Trade Commission (FTC) prior to the designated transfer date;

---

[3] These transferred authorities are found in sections 1061(b) and 1063 of the Dodd-Frank Act, which are effective on the designated transfer date.

**Joint Response by the Inspectors General of the Department of the Treasury and Board of Governors of the Federal Reserve System**

*Request for Information Regarding the Bureau of Consumer Financial Protection*

---

- conduct all consumer protection functions relating to the Real Estate Settlement Procedures Act of 1974, the Secure and Fair Enforcement for Mortgage Licensing Act of 2008, and the Interstate Land Sales Full Disclosure Act that were previously within the authority of the Secretary of the Department of Housing and Urban Development prior to the designated transfer date;

- enforce all orders, resolutions, determinations, agreements, and rulings that have been issued, made, prescribed, or allowed to become effective prior to the designated transfer date by any transferor agency or by a court of competent jurisdiction, in the performance of consumer financial protection functions that are transferred to the Bureau, with respect to a bank, savings association, or credit union with total assets in excess of $10 billion, and any affiliates thereof; and

- replace the Board, the Office of the Comptroller of the Currency, the Office of Thrift Supervision, the Federal Deposit Insurance Corporation, the National Credit Union Administration, and the Department of Housing and Urban Development in any lawsuit or proceeding that was commenced by or against one of the transferor agencies prior to the designated transfer date, with respect to a consumer financial protection function transferred to the Bureau.

Since subtitle F transfers the above functions to the Bureau on the designated transfer date, in the absence of a Senate-confirmed Director, the text of section 1066(a) authorizes the Secretary to perform these transferred functions. The Secretary's authority to carry out these transferred functions terminates when a Director is confirmed by the Senate.

In addition to the transferred functions, the Bureau has newly-established federal consumer financial regulatory authorities. The Secretary is not permitted to perform certain newly-established Bureau authorities if there is

**Joint Response by the Inspectors General of the Department of the Treasury and Board of Governors of the Federal Reserve System**

*Request for Information Regarding the Bureau of Consumer Financial Protection*

---

no confirmed Director by the designated transfer date.[4] For example, if there is no Senate-confirmed Director by the designated transfer date, in general, the Secretary is not permitted to exercise the Bureau's authority to:

- prohibit unfair, deceptive, or abusive acts or practices under subtitle C in connection with consumer financial products and services;

- prescribe rules and require model disclosure forms under subtitle C to ensure that the features of a consumer financial product or service are fairly, accurately, and effectively disclosed both initially and over the term of the product or service;

- prescribe rules under section 1022 relating to, among other things, the filing of limited reports to the Bureau for the purpose of determining whether a nondepository institution should be supervised by the Bureau;

- supervise nondepository institutions under section 1024, including the authority to (a) prescribe rules defining the scope of nondepository institutions subject to the Bureau's supervision, (b) prescribe rules establishing recordkeeping requirements that the Bureau determines are needed to facilitate nondepository supervision, and (c) conduct examinations of nondepository institutions.

6. *What appropriation account, or accounts, is the Treasury Department using to fund the work relating to the Bureau? How much does the Department estimate that this effort will cost in total?*

According to Treasury, funds from the Board, not from appropriation accounts, support the activities of the Bureau.[5] Treasury established a separate "Treasury General Account" to receive disbursements from a Board account, called the

---

[4] The Bureau's newly-established authorities are found throughout title X of the Dodd-Frank Act, including section 1024, and multiple provisions of section 1022 and subtitle C. According to the text of the Dodd-Frank Act, the Secretary's authority under section 1066(a) does not extend to these newly-established authorities.

[5] The Board is not funded through appropriations. 12 U.S.C. §§ 243-44.

**Joint Response by the Inspectors General of the Department of the Treasury and
Board of Governors of the Federal Reserve System**

*Request for Information Regarding the Bureau of Consumer Financial Protection*

---

Bureau Fund, which was established in accordance with the funding provisions set forth in the Dodd-Frank Act.[6] Thus far, the Bureau implementation team has made two requests to the Board for funds to support the activities to establish the Bureau – an initial request on August 11, 2010, for $18.4 million and a supplemental request on December 21, 2010, for $14.37 million.

Treasury officials stated that it would currently be very difficult to estimate the total cost of establishing the Bureau because that activity will span several years. We were told that the Bureau implementation team currently has a draft budget for Fiscal Year (FY) 2011 and FY 2012, which will be included in the President's FY 2012 budget request.

7. *Please provide a list of all employees of the Treasury Department, Board of Governors, and any other federal agency who since July 21, 2010, have performed, are performing, or are likely to perform any tasks relating in any way to establishing the Bureau and who are (a) serving in positions for which they were nominated by the President and confirmed by the Senate; (b) members of the Senior Executive Service; (c) Schedule C employees; or (d) paid at the GS-15 level or its equivalent.*

Treasury's Response:

The list below, provided by Treasury, includes: (1) Presidentially appointed, Senate-confirmed (PAS) officials within Treasury's Departmental Offices who have performed any task related to establishing the Bureau; (2) staff hired by Treasury to work full-time on establishing the Bureau; (3) Treasury employees detailed to work on implementation efforts; (4) other Treasury employees who spend 50 percent or more of their time on implementation activities; and (5) detailees assigned to Treasury from other federal or state agencies working on Bureau implementation.

---

[6] The Treasury General Account established for the Bureau is a no-year special receipts account in which the funds will remain available until expended.

**Joint Response by the Inspectors General of the Department of the Treasury and Board of Governors of the Federal Reserve System**

*Request for Information Regarding the Bureau of Consumer Financial Protection*

---

The list does not include *all* employees who "have performed, are performing, or are likely to perform any tasks relating in any way to establishing the Bureau" because, according to the Chief of Staff of the Bureau Implementation Team:

> "[T]he request would require Treasury to identify every qualifying employee who has received (or is likely to receive) even a single email related to the [Bureau] or has had (or is likely to have) even a single discussion related to the [Bureau]. No such list currently exists. And creating such a list, and confirming its accuracy, would require a significant amount of time and resources. Moreover, it would include numerous employees who have done very little work regarding the [Bureau]. For all these reasons, we submitted an alternative list . . . of all qualifying employees who have devoted a majority of their time, in various capacities, to establishing the Bureau."

With respect to Treasury PAS employees, Treasury stated that the list provided, given the broad scope of the requested information, includes every PAS official who has received an email related to the Bureau, had a discussion related to the Bureau, or attended a meeting at which the Bureau was discussed.

Additionally, the list below includes employees of the Board and other federal or state agencies that have been detailed to Treasury. According to the Chief of Staff of the Bureau Implementation Team, Treasury is unable to identify personnel from other agencies who may be working on Bureau issues but are not detailees.[7]

| Last Name | First Name | Category |
| --- | --- | --- |
| Allison | Herb | PAS (no longer with Treasury) |
| Barr | Michael | PAS (no longer with Treasury) |
| Brainard | Lael | PAS |
| Cohen | David | PAS |
| Collyns | Charles | PAS |

---

[7] If the Board OIG identifies personnel in other agencies who are working on Bureau issues, it will provide that information under a separate cover.

**Joint Response by the Inspectors General of the Department of the Treasury and Board of Governors of the Federal Reserve System**

*Request for Information Regarding the Bureau of Consumer Financial Protection*

| Last Name | First Name | Category |
|---|---|---|
| Geithner | Timothy | PAS |
| Goldstein | Jeffrey | PAS |
| Ireland | S. Leslie | PAS |
| Krueger | Alan | PAS (no longer with Treasury) |
| Lago | Marisa | PAS |
| Levey | Stuart | PAS |
| Madison | George | PAS |
| Miller | Mary | PAS |
| Mundaca | Michael | PAS |
| Rios | Rosie | PAS |
| Tangherlini | Daniel | PAS |
| Wallace | Kim | PAS |
| Wolin | Neal | PAS |
| Coloretti | Nani | Non-Career SES |
| Warren | Elizabeth | Non-Career SES |
| Horowitz | Linda | SES |
| Lepley | Rich | SES |
| Twohig | Peggy | SES |
| Antonakes | Steve | Limited Term SES |
| Dickman | Marilyn | Limited Term SES |
| Slagter | Dennis | Limited Term SES |
| Breslaw | April | SES Equivalent |
| Burniston | Tim | SES Equivalent |
| Campbell | Michael | SES Equivalent |
| Chow | Edwin | SES Equivalent |
| Hancock | Gary | SES Equivalent |
| Leiss | Wayne | SES Equivalent |
| Marshall | Mira | SES Equivalent |
| Gordon | Mike | Senior-Level |
| Adeyamo | Adewale | Schedule C/GS-14 |
| Goldfarb | Rachael | Schedule C/GS-15 |
| Cochran | Kelly | GS-15 |
| Coleman | John | GS-15 |

**Joint Response by the Inspectors General of the Department of the Treasury and Board of Governors of the Federal Reserve System**

*Request for Information Regarding the Bureau of Consumer Financial Protection*

| Last Name | First Name | Category |
|-----------|-----------|----------|
| Date | Rajeev | GS-15 |
| Galicki | Josh | GS-15 |
| Geldon | Dan | GS-15 |
| Hrdy | Alice | GS-15 |
| Huang | Eugene | GS-15 |
| Kershbaum | Sharon | GS-15 |
| Lev | Ori | GS-15 |
| Martinez | Adam | GS-15 |
| Martinez | Zixta | GS-15 |
| Morris | Lucy | GS-15 |
| Pluta | Scott | GS-15 |
| Reilly | Deborah | GS-15 |
| Royster | Felicia | GS-15 |
| Scanlon | Thomas | GS-15 |
| Silberman | David | GS-15 |
| Stapleton | Claire | GS-15 |
| Vale | Elizabeth | GS-15 |
| Cantrell | Diane | GS-15 Equivalent |
| Decker | Sharon | GS-15 Equivalent |
| Duncan | Tim | GS-15 Equivalent |
| McCoy | Patricia | GS-15 Equivalent |
| VanMeter | Stephen | GS-15 Equivalent |

Board's Response:

Many Board employees have been consulted on matters pertaining to the Bureau. The following is a list of Board employees who have or are performing a substantive role in tasks related to establishing the Bureau. Specifically, these individuals have been involved in matters relating to the transfer of functions and employees, retirement benefits issues, information sharing agreements, and information technology security issues.

**Joint Response by the Inspectors General of the Department of the Treasury and
Board of Governors of the Federal Reserve System**

*Request for Information Regarding the Bureau of Consumer Financial Protection*

| Last Name | First Name | Category |
|---|---|---|
| Duke | Elizabeth | PAS |
| Alvarez | Scott | SES Equivalent |
| Boutillier | Elaine | SES Equivalent |
| Braunstein | Sandra | SES Equivalent |
| Chanin | Leonard | SES Equivalent |
| Clark | Michell | SES Equivalent |
| Fox | Lynn | SES Equivalent |
| Glissman | Todd | SES Equivalent |
| Hammond | Donald | SES Equivalent |
| Mitchell | William | SES Equivalent |
| Price | Tonda | SES Equivalent |
| Riesz | James | SES Equivalent |
| Romero | Raymond | SES Equivalent |
| Tinsley Pelitere | Tara | SES Equivalent |
| Vassallo | Karen | SES Equivalent |
| Wheatley | Katherine | SES Equivalent |
| Acconero | Michael | GS-15 Equivalent |
| Anderson | Jean | GS-15 Equivalent |
| Delaney | Craig | GS-15 Equivalent |
| Eskow | Beverley | GS-15 Equivalent |
| Foster | Alye | GS-15 Equivalent |
| Kapoor | Michelle | GS-15 Equivalent |
| Richards | Brenda | GS-15 Equivalent |
| Roach | Reginald | GS-15 Equivalent |

8. *The Federal Deposit Insurance Corporation (FDIC), the Securities and Exchange Commission (SEC) and the Commodity Futures Trading Commission (CFTC) are publicly disclosing the names of all persons from outside government who meet with officials of those agencies with respect to implementation of the Act, as well as the subject matter of such meetings. Are the federal employees responsible for establishing the Bureau, including Professor Warren, complying with this protocol with respect to meetings regarding the Bureau and all related issues? If so, where is this information available? Has this information been*

**Joint Response by the Inspectors General of the Department of the Treasury and Board of Governors of the Federal Reserve System**

*Request for Information Regarding the Bureau of Consumer Financial Protection*

---

*disclosed with respect to meetings that have taken place since the President signed the Act into law on July 21?*

On November 1, 2010, Treasury announced a policy to disclose meetings regarding Dodd-Frank Act implementation (which includes Bureau-related activities) between certain Treasury officials and individuals from private sector entities and/or nongovernmental organizations.[8] The policy covers meetings attended by Treasury officials who are Deputy Assistant Secretaries or of equal or higher rank, including (1) Counselors to the Secretary and (2) Special Advisors to the Secretary, including Professor Warren. The policy also states that Treasury will respond to individual requests for information about meetings that occurred prior to November 1, 2010, through the standard Freedom of Information Act process.

In accordance with its policy, on December 30, 2010, Treasury released information on Dodd-Frank implementation meetings that occurred during the month of November 2010. The disclosure included the names and affiliations of all non-Treasury participants and a list of primary discussion topics. As of the date of our letter, the disclosure is at www.treasury.gov/initiatives/wsr/Pages/DoddFrank.aspx. Also, in response to a Freedom of Information Act request, Treasury posted to its website Professor Warren's schedule from September 20, 2010, through December 3, 2010.[9] Treasury plans to continue to post Professor Warren's schedule on a regular basis.

## B. Bureau Organizational Structure

1. *Have those responsible for organizing the Bureau studied the organizational and managerial criticisms of existing federal financial regulators and changes they have made to address these issues? Have they identified lessons learned from*

---

[8] The policy, "Treasury Policy on Voluntary Disclosure of Meetings on Dodd-Frank Implementation," can be found on Treasury's website at www.financialstability.gov/roadtostability/transparency.html.
[9] As of the date of our letter, Professor Warren's schedule was available at www.treasury.gov/FOIA/Pages/other-index.aspx.

**Joint Response by the Inspectors General of the Department of the Treasury and Board of Governors of the Federal Reserve System**

*Request for Information Regarding the Bureau of Consumer Financial Protection*

---

*the enforcement failures that plagued these agencies in recent years? How are they incorporating these lessons in designing the structure of the Bureau?*

According to Treasury, the Bureau implementation team has met with officials from a number of federal financial regulators and has studied their organizational structures and managerial frameworks.[10] The Bureau implementation team reported that it also met with officials from other recently created governmental entities, such as Treasury's Office of Financial Stability and the Federal Housing Finance Agency, to identify lessons learned and seek advice about how to avoid start-up pitfalls. Furthermore, Treasury commissioned (and received) a study that addressed lessons learned from previous federal mergers, stand-ups, and reorganizations. According to the Deputy Assistant Secretary for Management and Budget, the Bureau is incorporating a lesson learned from a recently established federal agency that experienced morale problems when it attempted to use six different payroll and compensation systems to pay employees performing the same function. As a result, the Bureau plans to implement a single payroll and compensation system prior to the transfer of employees from other agencies.

According to the Chief of Staff of the Bureau Implementation Team, the Bureau will continue to identify the lessons learned from regulatory enforcement failures. The Bureau implementation team is establishing a Memorandum of Understanding with each of the other regulatory agencies to gain access to the proprietary and restricted regulatory information associated with enforcement issues. Furthermore, Professor Warren said that she has identified several lessons learned that she is applying to the Bureau. For instance, she believes that in order to establish an effective enforcement and supervision function, an organization must have a strong culture, effectively communicate its mission, and maintain a coherent vision. According to Professor Warren, it is important that senior leadership support "line-level" employees, including delegating sufficient authority to complete assigned duties and responsibilities. In addition,

---

[10] These federal financial regulators include the Board, Office of the Comptroller of the Currency, Office of Thrift Supervision, Federal Deposit Insurance Corporation, Federal Trade Commission, and National Credit Union Administration.

**Joint Response by the Inspectors General of the Department of the Treasury and Board of Governors of the Federal Reserve System**

*Request for Information Regarding the Bureau of Consumer Financial Protection*

---

Professor Warren stated that regulators need to "maintain distance" from the institutions they are examining.

2. *Is there a plan for the Bureau's organizational structure? What divisions or offices are being considered? Has a draft organizational plan or draft budget been prepared? If so, please describe the process for obtaining public comment with respect to such drafts. If a draft organizational plan and budget have not yet been prepared, please describe the process for preparing them, including the persons responsible, the factors and models being considered, and whether and how public input will be sought with respect to a draft organizational plan and budget.*

The Bureau implementation team currently has a draft plan of the Bureau's organizational structure and a draft budget for FY 2011 and FY 2012. A December 8, 2010, draft of the Bureau's organizational structure indicates that, in addition to administrative divisions and offices, the Bureau is considering three mission-related directorates: Education and Engagement; Supervision and Enforcement; and Research, Markets, and Rules. According to Treasury officials, the organizational plan is a "work-in-progress," and the Bureau implementation team expects to continue modifying the plan going forward. Treasury officials also stated that the Bureau implementation team's draft budgets for FY 2011 and FY 2012 will be included in the President's FY 2012 request, which traditionally is released at the end of January or beginning of February.

Regarding the solicitation of public input, Treasury does not have a formal process to obtain feedback regarding the draft organizational plan and draft budget. However, Professor Warren stated that she regularly seeks input from federal agencies, industry participants, and other stakeholders during informal discussions. In addition, the Bureau plans to include an online forum for public input on its website, which it intends to launch by the end of January 2011.

3. *How will the Bureau's structure address the need to ensure that regulations, examinations, and enforcement strategies do not lead to a further reduction in the availability or affordability of credit for small businesses and consumers?*

**Joint Response by the Inspectors General of the Department of the Treasury and Board of Governors of the Federal Reserve System**

*Request for Information Regarding the Bureau of Consumer Financial Protection*

---

The Bureau implementation team plans to include an Office of Small Business and Community Banks within the Bureau's organizational structure. In addition, the Bureau's draft organizational chart includes a Research, Markets, and Rules division that, according to Treasury, comprises three components: a research team that studies consumer behavior and product risks; a rulemaking team that drafts rules, interpretations, and guidance; and a markets team that focuses on understanding and monitoring markets for individual products, such as mortgages, credit cards, and student loans. The Bureau implementation team expects that these teams will work together to ensure that policy initiatives are tailored to identified problems and that any policy initiatives that affect consumer risk, affordability, and access are appropriately estimated.

4. *Despite an infusion of at least $500 million in Federal funds, the Bureau will be subject to little or no oversight of how such money is spent. What internal processes and mechanisms will be in place to safeguard against waste, fraud and abuse?*

As discussed in our answer to Question A.6., Treasury reported that the Bureau implementation team made two requests to the Board for funds to support the activities to establish the Bureau – an initial request on August 11, 2010, for $18.4 million and a supplemental request on December 21, 2010, for $14.37 million.[11] The Bureau implementation team follows existing Treasury internal controls policies and procedures for financial activities such as contracting, purchase requests, and disbursements. In addition, Treasury officials stated that the Bureau of the Public Debt's Administrative Resource Center (ARC) provides the Bureau with financial management services to ensure that financial systems and processes comply with federal laws and regulations.[12] The Bureau implementation team is in the process of developing the Bureau's policies and procedures and determining whether to continue using ARC or implement a different financial management system after the designated transfer date.

---

[11] According to section 1017(c) of the Dodd-Frank Act, the funds transferred from the Board to the Bureau are not government funds or appropriated monies.
[12] ARC provides administrative services such as financial management to various federal agencies, including the Bureau implementation team.

**Joint Response by the Inspectors General of the Department of the Treasury and Board of Governors of the Federal Reserve System**

*Request for Information Regarding the Bureau of Consumer Financial Protection*

---

The ongoing independent oversight provided by the OIGs is another means for safeguarding against waste, fraud, and abuse within the Bureau's programs and operations. Additionally, the new Bureau will be subject to external oversight by Congress and others. For example, the Government Accountability Office (GAO) is responsible for conducting an annual audit of the financial transactions of the Bureau in accordance with generally accepted government auditing standards, and the Bureau is required to provide GAO with an assertion as to the effectiveness of its internal controls for financial reporting.

C. Bureau Regulatory Agenda

1. *Is the Treasury Secretary, his designee or anyone else, empowered to exercise the Bureau's rulemaking authority prior to the designated transfer date? If so, will any proposed rules, final rules, or advanced notices of proposed rulemaking be issued prior to the designated transfer date (if possible, please identify the topics those rules will address or identify the date or dates by which those topics will be identified). Is there a plan for the Secretary or his designee to solicit public input before formulating a proposed rule by, for example, issuing advanced notices of proposed rulemaking, as other agencies implementing the Act have done?*

The Treasury Secretary is not authorized to prescribe rules under the Bureau's rulemaking authority prior to the designated transfer date.[13] Until that date, rulemaking authority under federal consumer financial law remains with the federal regulatory agencies that currently have such rulemaking responsibilities.[14] However, if confirmed by the Senate, the Director of the

---

[13] Subtitle F of title X of the Dodd-Frank Act, which describes the Secretary's interim authority, does not include a provision that authorizes the Secretary to issue rules prior to the designated transfer date under the Bureau's authority. In addition, since the Secretary is not authorized to prescribe rules prior to the designated transfer date, the Secretary cannot delegate this authority to a designee.

[14] The provisions of the Dodd-Frank Act that transfer rulemaking authority to the Bureau are found in subtitles F and H of title X, and these provisions do not become effective until the designated transfer date.

**Joint Response by the Inspectors General of the Department of the Treasury and Board of Governors of the Federal Reserve System**

*Request for Information Regarding the Bureau of Consumer Financial Protection*

---

Bureau is granted a limited amount of rulemaking authority prior to the designated transfer date,[15] to include, among other things:

- conditional or unconditional exemptions of certain individuals, institutions, or consumer financial products or services from the Bureau-related provisions of the Dodd-Frank Act;[16]

- the process for gathering information from individuals or institutions participating in the consumer financial services markets;[17]

- the filing of limited reports to the Bureau for the purpose of determining whether a nondepository institution should be supervised and regulated by the Bureau;[18]

- the confidential treatment of information obtained from persons in connection with an exercise of the Bureau's authority;[19]

- the process for registering persons that participate in the consumer financial services markets (other than insured depository institutions, credit unions, or related persons);[20]

---

[15] Rulemaking authority for the "Federal consumer financial laws" was provided to the Director under section 1022 of the Dodd-Frank Act. Prior to the designated transfer date, this rulemaking authority for the "Federal consumer financial laws" applies to the provisions of the Dodd-Frank Act that are effective as of enactment. Prior to the designated transfer date, the Director's rulemaking authority does not include (1) those laws that must be transferred to the Bureau from the other federal regulators, or (2) the newly-established Bureau authorities found under subtitle C. Under sections 1061(d) and 1037, the rulemaking authority related to these provisions is effective on the designated transfer date.

[16] Section 1022(b)(3).

[17] Section 1022(c)(4).

[18] Section 1022(c)(5).

[19] Section 1022(c)(6)(A).

[20] Section 1022(c)(7)(A).

**Joint Response by the Inspectors General of the Department of the Treasury and Board of Governors of the Federal Reserve System**

*Request for Information Regarding the Bureau of Consumer Financial Protection*

- the scope of nondepository institutions subject to the supervision and regulation of the Bureau, which must be issued in consultation with the FTC;[21] and

- the process of recordkeeping and other informational requirements that the Bureau determines are needed to facilitate the supervision of nondepository persons and institutions, which must be issued in consultation with state agencies.[22]

While the Secretary is not authorized to prescribe rules prior to the designated transfer date, Treasury is considering whether it will issue advance notices of proposed rulemaking (ANPRs), which according to Treasury, do not contain substantive rules, but are "a means of gathering information and input, before the transfer date." Treasury has not yet made a decision regarding the content or timing of any such potential ANPRs.

According to Treasury officials, the Bureau implementation team is using informal channels, including public forums and meetings with industry representatives, to collect information regarding the Bureau's rulemaking considerations. In addition, the Bureau implementation team intends to include a page on the Bureau website, which is planned to be launched by the end of January 2011, where the public can provide its input on any number of topics relating to the Bureau.

2. *Will priorities be identified prior to the designated transfer date with respect to rulemaking proceedings to be undertaken by the Bureau after the designated transfer date? Who is responsible for identifying those priorities? What considerations will be taken into account in identifying those priorities? Is there a plan to seek public input with respect to those priorities?*

Professor Warren and the Bureau implementation team are in the process of identifying priorities for rulemaking proceedings to be undertaken after the

---

[21] Section 1024(a)(2).
[22] Section 1024(b)(7).

**Joint Response by the Inspectors General of the Department of the Treasury and Board of Governors of the Federal Reserve System**

*Request for Information Regarding the Bureau of Consumer Financial Protection*

designated transfer date. Professor Warren told us that cost savings, improved regulatory compliance, and simplified consumer disclosures are among the factors being considered in establishing the rulemaking priorities. In addition, Professor Warren and members of the Bureau implementation team have met with staff from the financial regulatory agencies that will be transferring rulemaking authority to the Bureau in an effort to better understand existing regulatory priorities. Professor Warren provided examples of two policy initiatives that will receive priority: (1) consolidating duplicate and overlapping mortgage disclosure forms mandated by the Truth in Lending Act and the Real Estate Settlement Procedures Act and (2) simplifying credit card agreements to ensure that customers fully understand fees and finance charges.

Professor Warren has informally collected public input through meetings with industry representatives and consumer groups. In addition, according to Treasury, Bureau officials are continuing to meet with members of the public to obtain input with respect to rulemaking priorities. The Bureau also intends to collect public input through its website, which it plans to launch by the end of January 2011.

3. *Does the Treasury Secretary, his designee, or anyone else have the power to order supervisory examinations prior to the designated transfer date?*

The Treasury Secretary is not authorized to conduct supervisory examinations prior to the designated transfer date.[23] Until that date, consumer compliance examinations may be conducted by the regulatory agencies that have examination authority under current law.[24] However, during the interim period, the Secretary may exercise the Bureau's authority to have Bureau examiners

---

[23] Subtitle F of title X of the Dodd-Frank Act, which describes the Secretary's interim authority, does not include a provision that authorizes the Treasury Secretary to order supervisory examinations prior to the designated transfer date. In addition, since the Treasury Secretary is not authorized to order examinations prior to the designated transfer date, the Treasury Secretary cannot delegate this authority to a designee.

[24] The provisions of the Dodd-Frank Act that transfer rulemaking, examination, and other authorities to the Bureau are found in subtitles F and H of title X, and these provisions do not become effective until the designated transfer date.

**Joint Response by the Inspectors General of the Department of the Treasury and Board of Governors of the Federal Reserve System**

*Request for Information Regarding the Bureau of Consumer Financial Protection*

---

participate (on a sampling basis) in the current regulators' compliance examinations of depository institutions with total assets greater than $10 billion, and any affiliate thereof. In addition, if nominated by the President and confirmed by the Senate, the Director is authorized to conduct supervisory examinations of nondepository institutions prior to the designated transfer date.[25]

4. *Will priorities be identified prior to the designated transfer date with respect to enforcement proceedings to be undertaken by the Bureau after the designated transfer date? Who is responsible for identifying those priorities? What considerations will be taken into account in identifying those priorities? Is there a plan to seek public input with respect to those priorities?*

    According to Treasury, the Bureau implementation team is developing plans, policies, procedures, and staffing levels for the Bureau's enforcement function. While the Bureau has not yet established priorities for enforcement activities that will be undertaken after the designated transfer date, the recent hiring of implementation team leaders for (1) enforcement and (2) nondepository and depository supervision will enhance the priority-setting process. Professor Warren stated that she will make sure that lessons learned from other regulatory agencies are considered as the Bureau sets its enforcement priorities. With regard to public input, Professor Warren said that she derives insights from meetings with industry, consumer groups, and citizens. She noted that she plans to collect public input on enforcement issues through the Bureau's website, which is planned to be launched by the end of January 2011.

5. *Several provisions of the Act require coordination between the Bureau and the Federal Trade Commission (FTC). Have discussions taken place with regard to this coordination? Have decisions been made regarding the considerations that will be taken into account in determining how to coordinate the activities of these two agencies? Is there a plan to seek public input with respect to this issue?*

---

[25] The Director's authority to examine nondepository institutions is found in section 1024 of the Dodd-Frank Act, and this provision became effective on the date of enactment.

**Joint Response by the Inspectors General of the Department of the Treasury and Board of Governors of the Federal Reserve System**

*Request for Information Regarding the Bureau of Consumer Financial Protection*

---

Professor Warren stated that coordination with FTC has occurred at all levels, and that she regularly speaks with the FTC Chairman. In addition, the Bureau implementation team and FTC staff are discussing the status and timing of the rulemaking authority that will transfer to the Bureau. Coordination on enforcement issues has not yet begun. However, Professor Warren said the Bureau implementation team intends to begin developing a specific coordination plan that will include a Memorandum of Understanding that addresses topics such as enforcement, consumer financial products and services, consumer complaints, and civil actions. The Bureau implementation team and FTC have also discussed coordination issues during meetings of an interagency working group comprised of representatives from each of the federal regulatory agencies that will be transferring consumer protection functions to the Bureau.[26]

According to a Treasury official, there is no formal plan to seek public input regarding coordination with FTC; however, coordination issues are addressed during meetings between the Bureau implementation team (including Professor Warren) and the public. In addition, Professor Warren stated that the new Bureau website will include a mechanism for public input on any Bureau-related issue, and that the Bureau plans to launch its website in late January 2011.

---

[26] The participating agencies in the interagency working group are the Board, Office of the Comptroller of the Currency, Office of Thrift Supervision, Federal Deposit Insurance Corporation, National Credit Union Association, Department of Housing and Urban Development, and FTC.

Interagency Agreement

between

The United States Department of the Treasury

and

the Board of Governors of the Federal Reserve System

for Providing Funds for the Bureau of Consumer Financial Protection


I.  Background & Purpose

The Board of Governors of the Federal Reserve System ("Board") and the United States
Department of the Treasury ("Agency") hereby enter into this Interagency Agreement
("Agreement") for the creation and operation of the Bureau of Consumer Financial Protection
Fund from the date of this Agreement through the designated transfer date (as hereinafter
defined) (the "Project"). Throughout this Agreement, the Board and the Agency may be
collectively referred to as the "Parties."

II.  Authority

The Board enters into this Agreement pursuant to its authority under Section 10 of the
Federal Reserve Act (12 U.S.C. § 244). The Agency enters into this Agreement and the account
agreement referenced in this Agreement pursuant to its authority under Section 1017 of the
Dodd-Frank Wall Street Reform and Consumer Protection Act (the "Act") .

III.  Scope of Work & Division of Responsibilities

The Parties hereby agree their respective responsibilities shall be as follows:

A.  Board

    1.  Transfer of funds into the Bureau Fund Account. The Board shall, in accordance
    with this Agreement, establish an account at the Federal Reserve Bank of New
    York ("FRBNY") designated the Bureau of Consumer Financial Protection Fund
    Account (the "Bureau Fund Account") and transfer funds to the Bureau Fund
    Account as directed by the Secretary of the Treasury or his authorized designee
    identified below in section III.B.4. (collectively, the "Secretary"). The Board will
    use its best efforts to accomplish such transfers promptly. It is the expectation of
    the parties that funds requested by 10:00 am Eastern Standard Time on a business
    day will be transferred to the Bureau Fund Account within 3 business days of the
    Board's receipt of a request from the Secretary, but the Board shall have no
    liability under this Agreement in the event that a transfer is delayed. The Board

will notify the Agency promptly when it has effected a transfer to the Bureau Fund Account.

2. Disbursements from the Bureau Fund Account. The Board shall require FRBNY to make disbursements from the Bureau Fund Account. Disbursements will be allowed only as provided for under Section III.B.2, below.

3. Investments. On request of the Secretary, or his authorized designee, the Board may direct FRBNY to invest funds in the Bureau Fund Account that are not immediately required to meet the current needs of the Bureau. The Board will transmit investment requests to FRBNY within one full business day of receipt of such requests. The Board has no responsibility or liability for FRBNY's action or inaction upon receipt of such instructions.

B. Agency

1. Transfer of funds into the Bureau Fund Account. The Secretary shall notify the Board of amounts he estimates are needed to carry out the authorities granted to the Bureau of Consumer Financial Protection until the designated transfer date as provided for in Title X of the Act (the "designated transfer date").

2. Disbursements from the Bureau Fund Account. The Secretary may direct disbursements from the Bureau Fund Account in writing in a form and manner acceptable to the FRBNY, with simultaneous notice to the Board. The Secretary shall comply with such rules as the Board or the FRBNY may direct relating to authentication of instructions. Amounts disbursed from the Bureau Fund Account will be deposited into the Treasury General Account or such other account as may be designated in writing by the Secretary or the individuals authorized to make disbursements in Section III.B.4.C below. FRBNY reserves the right to limit disbursements to one transfer per day if in its sole discretion disbursement requests are received too frequently.

3. Investments. The Secretary shall make investment requests of the FRBNY, with simultaneous notice to the Board, in accordance with the attached automatic investment program letter (Attachment C). The Secretary shall comply with such rules as the Board or the FRBNY may direct relating to authentication of instructions. The FRBNY shall invest Bureau funds only in investments that are eligible for investment under Section 1017(b)(3)(B) of the Act. The Board shall have no liability for any investment direction made by the Secretary.

4. Authority to take Actions on Behalf of the Secretary. For actions taken under this section III. B., the Secretary hereby designates the listed individuals below to act in his place and with his authority under the Act. These officials will provide such identification as required by the Board or the FRBNY when taking action under this Agreement.

A. For all purposes arising under the Project the following individuals may act on behalf of the Secretary:

1. Dan Tangherlini, Assistant Secretary for Management and Chief Financial Officer
2. Adewale (Wally) Adeyemo, Deputy Executive Secretary
3. Nani Coloretti, Deputy Asst. Secretary for Management and Budget
4. Elizabeth Erickson, detailee (Implementation CFO)

B. For any transfer instruction under III.B.1, the following individuals may act on behalf of the Secretary:

1. Dorrice Roth, Director, Office of Financial Management (OFM)
2. David M. Legge, Associate Director for Accounting, OFM

C. For disbursement instructions under III.B.2. the following individuals may act on behalf of the Secretary:

1. Dorrice Roth, Director, Office of Financial Management (OFM)
2. David M. Legge, Associate Director for Accounting, OFM

D. For investment instructions under III.B.3. the following individuals may act on behalf of the Secretary:

1. Dorrice Roth, Director, Office of Financial Management (OFM)
2. David M. Legge, Associate Director for Accounting, OFM

IV.   Rules Governing the Bureau Fund Account

A. The Bureau Fund Account shall be located at the FRBNY and shall be established and maintained in accordance with rules the Board establishes, including the attached Account Agreement as well as the attached Terms of Service and other such account operating documents as may be used by FRBNY from time to time in the course of its business.

B. FRBNY shall provide the Agency with electronic access to daily account information showing the activity of the Bureau Fund Account, such as the account balance, deposits, withdrawals, and similar financial transactions.

C. The Agency shall be solely responsible for tracking and accounting for all monies in the Bureau Fund Account to ensure that they are used solely for the purpose of carrying out the authorities granted to the Bureau of Consumer Financial Protection under Federal consumer financial laws (as that term is defined in the Act) from the date of enactment of the Act until the designated transfer date. Any monies or securities in the Bureau Fund Account at the opening of business on the designated transfer date shall remain in the Bureau Fund Account. The Parties agree that during the fiscal year in which the designated transfer date occurs, the total amount of funds requested under section 1017(a)(1) of the Act and the balance of funds (cash and securities) remaining in the Bureau Fund Account on the designated transfer date shall not exceed the funding cap established under section 1017(a)(2) of the Act. The Board and FRBNY shall maintain the confidentiality of the Bureau Fund Account in accordance with the attached Account Agreement. Any requests for information pertaining to the Bureau Fund Account shall be forwarded to the Agency for a response. The Parties understand and agree that the Government Accountability Office, or its agents or contractors, may audit the Bureau Fund Account and may have such access to account information and all other information relating to the Bureau Fund Account as permitted by law.

D. Except as may be otherwise expressly agreed upon in writing, the Board shall assume no responsibility for any loss incurred by the Agency in connection with any services provided by the Board to the Agency under this Agreement, except to the extent that such loss has been caused by the Board's gross negligence or intentional misconduct. In circumstances where the Board is liable, the Board's liability shall be limited to direct losses, and shall not include incidental or consequential damages. The Board assumes no responsibility for any delay or failure to perform an obligation that is caused by events beyond the Board's reasonable control.

E. The Board and the FRBNY may require such procedures relating to authentication of authority to direct transactions under section III.B as the Board and the FRBNY, in their discretion, deem appropriate.

V. Term, Termination & Modification

A. This Agreement shall be effective as of the date last executed below and remain in effect until the earlier of the designated transfer date or until terminated as provided below. However, the Secretary's authority, as well as the authority of all of his designees, who are not employees of the Bureau, to take any action, other than an action to request funds, with respect to the Bureau Fund Account shall terminate as of the date on which a Director of the Bureau is confirmed by the Senate (in accordance with section 1011 of the Act), even if this Agreement continues in effect after that confirmation.

B. Notwithstanding any other provision of this Agreement, the Parties may terminate the Agreement at any time by mutual written agreement, provided, however, that the Bureau Fund Account shall continue in existence notwithstanding the termination of this Agreement.

C. Any modification of this Agreement must be accomplished by mutual written agreement, signed by persons authorized to act on behalf of the Parties.

VI.    Costs & Payment Provisions

The Board will not charge the Agency or assess fees for any actions governed by this Agreement. The Agency agrees to pay to the FRBNY such fees for the Bureau Account as may be called for in the Account Agreement and Terms of Service.

VII.    Other Applicable Laws

Throughout the term of this Agreement, Parties shall ensure that the Project complies with all applicable federal laws, regulations, policies, and guidelines, including but not limited to those regarding information security, access and privacy as applicable to the Parties. The determination as to applicability of laws, regulations, policies and guidelines shall be made by the Parties (and any disagreement shall be resolved in accordance with the Dispute Resolution provision of this Agreement).

VIII.    Notice & Contact Information

A. Except as provided in Section III paragraph B, any written notice that is required by this Agreement shall be sent by electronic means to the Parties as follows:

1. For the Board:

William L. Mitchell
Chief Financial Officer
Board of Governors of the Federal Reserve System
20th & C Streets NW, Mail Stop 152
Washington, DC 20551
Fax:        202-452-6490
Email      bill.mitchell@frb.gov

with copies to:

Elaine M. Boutilier
Deputy Associate Director
Board of Governors of the Federal Reserve System
20th & C Streets, NW, Mail Stop 128
Washington, DC 20551
Fax        202-728-5826
Email      elaine.boutilier@frb.gov

2. For the Agency:

Nani Coloretti
Deputy Assistant Secretary for Management and Budget
U.S. Department of the Treasury
1500 Pennsylvania Ave., NW

Washington, DC 20220
Tel      202-622-0016
Email    mani.coloretti@do.treas.gov

3. For the FRBNY:

Timothy J. Fogarty
Vice President
Central Bank and International Account Services[
33 Liberty Street
New York, N.Y. 10045
Fax      212-720-6331
Tel      212-720-1708
Email    timothy.fogarty@ny.frb.org  and
         account.relations@ny.frb.org

with copies to:  William Mitchell

B. For any transaction instruction under section III.B, the Agency's primary contacts at
the Board or FRBNY, as applicable, are as follows:

1. For purposes of transfer of funds into the Bureau Fund Account, William
Mitchell (contact information above), with copies to:

Craig Delaney
Manager, Accounting
Board of Governors of the Federal Reserve System
20th & C Streets NW, Mail Stop 152
Washington, DC 20551
Fax      202-452-6490
Email    Craig.J.Delaney@frb.gov

and:

Brenda L. Richards
Manager
Financial Accounting Section
Division of Reserve Bank Operations
Board of Governors of the Federal Reserve System
20th & C Streets, N.W., Mail Stop 193
Washington, DC 20551
Email:   Brenda.Richards@frb.gov

2. For purposes of disbursement instructions:

Central Bank and International Account Services[
33 Liberty Street
New York, N.Y. 10045
Fax        212-720-6331
Tel        212-720-5679
Email      account.relations@ny.frb.org

and:

Amelia Moncayo, Officer
Tel        212-720-1391
Email      amelia.moncayo@ny.frb.org

and:

Orson Keeys, Manager
Tel        804-698-7024
Email      orson.keeys@ny.frb.org

with copies to:   William L. Mitchell

3. For purposes of investment instructions:

Amelia Moncayo, Officer
Tel        212-720-1391
Email      amelia.moncayo@ny.frb.org

and:

Orson Keeys, Manager
Tel        804-698-7024
Email      orson.keeys@ny.frb.org

with copies to:

Donald Hammond
Deputy Director, Division of Reserve Bank Operations
 and Payment Systems
Board of Governors of the Federal Reserve System
20th & C Streets, N.W., Mail Stop 194
Washington, DC 20551
Tel        202-452-3660
Email      Donald.Hammond@frb.gov

and:

Brenda Richards
Manager
Financial Accounting Section
Division of Reserve Bank Operations
Board of Governors of the Federal Reserve System
20th & C Streets, N.W., Mail Stop 193
Washington, DC 20551
Email     Brenda.Richards@frb.gov

4.  For legal issues:

Jean Anderson
Senior Counsel
Legal Division
Board of Governors of the Federal Reserve System
20th & C Streets, N.W., Mail Stop 11A
Washington, DC 20551
Fax       202-736-5615
Email     Jean.Anderson@frb.gov

with copies to:

Katherine Wheatley
Associate General Counsel
Legal Division
Board of Governors of the Federal Reserve System
20th & C Streets, N.W., Mail Stop 12
Washington, DC 20551
Fax       202-736-5615
Email     Kit.Wheatley@frb.gov

C.  Notwithstanding any other provision herein, either Party may unilaterally change its respective contact(s) listed in this Section VIII of the Agreement by giving the other Party written notice of the change.

IX.     Dispute Resolution

In the event of any disagreement arising between the Parties concerning this Agreement, the Parties shall use their best efforts to negotiate a resolution in good faith.  If the disagreement cannot be resolved at the staff level, the Parties agree to elevate the matter to their respective appropriate higher officials.

X.   Counterparts/Facsimile

This Agreement may be executed as a facsimile and any number of counterparts, each of which when executed and delivered shall be deemed an original, and such counterparts together shall constitute one and the same instrument. For purposes hereof, any facsimile copy of this Agreement including the signature pages bearing the Parties' signatures shall be deemed an original.

XI.   Effective Date

This Agreement shall not be effective until it has been executed by each of the Parties and acknowledged by the FRBNY. When it has been so executed and acknowledged, this Agreement shall become effective on the date of the latest signature.

IN WITNESS WHEREOF, the Parties hereto have executed this Agreement on the day and year set forth below and do each hereby warrant and represent that their respective signatories, whose signatures appear below, have been and are on the date hereof duly authorized to execute this Agreement.

Board of Governors of the Federal Reserve System          Date:

By: _William L. Mitchell_          11/12/10
William L. Mitchell
Chief Financial Officer


United States Department
Of the Treasury                                          Date:

By: _Timothy F. Geithner_          11/4/2010
Timothy F. Geithner
Secretary of the Treasury


Acknowledged by:

Federal Reserve Bank of New York                        Date:

Name  TIMOTHY J FOGARTY          11/18/2010
Title  VICE PRESIDENT

Page 9 of 10

Attachments:

Attachment A:  Account Agreement
Attachment B:  Terms of Service
Attachment C:  Automatic Investment Program Letter